Editor
Emily R. Smith, M.A. Ed.

Editorial Manager
Elizabeth Morris, Ph.D.

Editor-in-Chief
Sharon Coan, M.S. Ed.

Illustrator
Ben DeSoto

Cover Design
Jeff Sutherland

Cover Artist
José Tapia

Photo Credit
Digital Imagery © copyright
2000 Corel, Inc.

Art Coordinator
Denice Adorno

Imaging
Ralph Olmedo, Jr.

Product Manager
Phil Garcia

Published in partnership with
Ready Ed Publications
11/17 Foley Street
Balcatta WA 6021
Australia
www.readyed.com.au

Publishers
Rachelle Cracchiolo, M.S. Ed.
Mary Dupuy Smith, M.S. Ed.

Internet Quests
CREEPY CRAWLIES

Primary

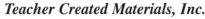

Author

Kellie Lloyd

Teacher Created Materials, Inc.
6421 Industry Way
Westminster, CA 92683
www.teachercreated.com
ISBN-0-7439-3408-3
©2001 Teacher Created Materials, Inc.
Made in U.S.A.

Table of Contents

Introduction

How to Use This Book

1. Internet Activity Pages

Note: As this is not an introductory book on using the Internet, you will need to have some understanding of how to navigate the World Wide Web and how to open various Internet addresses prior to attempting these Internet-related activities.

To make use of the pages headed **Internet Activity Pages**, access the Teacher Created Materials World Wide Web site at the following address:

http://www.teachercreated.com/books/3408
(Bookmark this site for easy access later.)

When the page opens in your browser, you will see a listing of page numbers and links to Web site addresses. If you click on one of the provided links, you will be taken to the Web page without having to laboriously type the address.

The CD-ROM included with this book also contains hyperlinks that will automatically connect you to the Web sites on the Internet.

2. Alternet Activity Pages

To make use of the pages headed **Alternet Activity Pages**, insert the Alternet CD into your computer's CD-ROM drive. The HTML files on the Alternet CD-ROM require either *Microsoft Internet Explorer* or *Netscape Navigator* to run, so you will need to access one or the other of these browsers. The CD-ROM contains the Alternet package relevant to this book.

The minimum hardware requirement for use of the Alternet program is any computer that uses a frame-capable browser. This includes both Macintosh® and Windows® operating systems.

---

3. How to Use the Alternet Program

The Alternet CD can be used on both Windows or Macintosh computers. Although you will need a browser to view the files, the computer does not need to be connected to the Internet, as all files are self-contained.

You may use the files directly from the CD by clicking on the *Creepy Crawlies* folder and then opening the file called [*begin.htm*]. For faster operation you can copy the contents of the *Creepy Crawlies* folder to a folder on your hard disk, remove the CD for safekeeping, then open [*begin.htm*] on your hard disk.

It is recommended that you create a new folder for the Alternet set from each book you have purchased (*Plants, Animals,* etc.). Name the folder after the book you are using.

Note: When you load the Alternet program for your students to use, the browser may give warning messages about connection difficulties. This is because you are not attempting to connect to the Internet. You can ignore this by clicking OK.

Note: Purchase of a single book gives you the right to copy the Alternet program on up to ten computers.

Teachers' Notes

Teacher Information

This series is designed to provide teachers of primary-aged children with a multimedia-based set of resources for the Creepy Crawlies theme.

In using this multimedia resource, students will be required to learn and utilize a range of associated skills such as:

- reading and interpreting given information.
- summarizing given information.
- using generalizations based on given information.
- navigating their way around a Web site.

What does this multimedia approach consist of?

This series aims to provide teachers with a three-pronged approach to meeting the requirements of concepts related to scientific research curriculum. It combines the use of traditional information sources such as reference books and materials with the enormous information capabilities of the Internet and the appeal of computer databases as provided by our Alternet program. As many schools face practical limitations in trying to make use of information accessed through the Internet and computer software, the materials provided here are aimed at having the class working as three groups, each using different methods of information retrieval, which eases the pressures on the available hardware and facilities.

1. The Internet

The use of the related activity pages in this book (titled **Internet Activity Pages**), together with the information sources provided by the World Wide Web, lends a contemporary and exciting aspect to studies in this subject area. As detailed on page 3 of this book, students access the relevant Web pages through the *Teacher Created Materials* Web site and use the information they find to complete the associated tasks on the activity pages.

2. The Alternet Program

The Alternet is a database of information and pictures related to the strand of study on which students are working. Its appearance emulates Web sites found on the Internet's World Wide Web and it is navigated in exactly the same way as the Web through the use of browsers. As with the Internet activities described above, students use the information gathered from the files to complete the relevant activity pages in this book (titled **Alternet Activity Pages**).

3. General Activities

For the activity pages in these sections (titled **General Activity Pages**), students utilize traditional print-related reference materials to complete the tasks on the sheets. It would be useful for a collection of appropriate books to be assembled before commencing the unit so these can be accessed and used with as little disruption as possible. Alternatively, Web site references have been included where possible to provide background information for teachers.

Teachers' Notes *(cont.)*

Updating and Checking of Internet Addresses

The dynamic nature of the Internet means that some sites may change URLs or even disappear altogether. An ongoing role of the publishers will be to monitor changes and post them on our Web site. All addresses used are checked weekly and changes will be posted on our Web site: **http://www.teachercreated.com/books/3408**.

Suggested Use of This Series

As indicated, a multimedia approach has been utilized not only to provide students with a range of reference sources but also to take account of the difficulties schools have in trying to match limited resource access with the requirements of the curriculum. To help teachers plan for these contingencies, this book has been structured to allow units of work where groups rotate from one information source to the next on a week-to-week basis.

It is important to note that the activities in each section are "stand-alone," meaning that students will not need to complete previous activities in order to work successfully. Exactly how teachers choose to use the materials is obviously dependent on the amount of computer hardware and Internet access available, but with a bare minimum in mind, books have been designed to allow a rotation (assuming one period per week is spent on the unit).

To help follow a planning pattern such as this, the following checklist can be used to check off the activity sheets that each group has completed:

1. Where possible, units are evenly balanced as in the example below, i.e., there is an equivalent number of Internet, Alternet, and print research activities in each section of the book to allow for easy rotation of groups.

2. Activity pages are designed to take about 25–30 minutes—the approximate length of time usually available in a school period after preliminaries have been sorted out.

Check List

Internet	Groups 1	2	3
What is an Insect?			
Insect Body Parts			
Insects A–Z			
The Life of a Butterfly			
A Louse and Some Lice			
Roach World			
EEK . . . a Spider!			
Nice Legs!			
The Most Wanted			
Get This Bug Off Of Me!			

Alternet	Groups 1	2	3
Bug Study			
Spider or Insect?			
Beautiful Beetles			
Ladybug, Ladybug			
Busy Bees			
The Ants Go Marching			
Hoppy To Know You			
The Good, Bad, and Creepy			
Yummy Bugs			
Interesting Insects			

General	Groups 1	2	3
Which One is an Insect?			
Home Sweet Home			
The Same on Both Sides			
Bug Collection			
Bug Search			
Cross-Bug Puzzle			
Stop Bugging Me!			
My Favorite Insect			
New Insect Discovered!			
Bug Power!			

The Insect World

Content Area(s):

- language
- science
- technology

Objectives:

In this section students:

- navigate their way around Web sites and find required information.
- label various insect parts.
- color various insect parts.
- identify an insect for each letter of the alphabet.

Materials Required:

- computer with Internet access
- pencil or pen

Web Site(s):

- Students need to access the TCM Web page for the Creepy Crawlies book at:

http://www.teachercreated.com/books/3408

- Students then click on the link to the page on which they are working.
- Allow the children time to familiarize themselves with the Web site before starting the activity sheets.

Time:

- Approximately 30 minutes per lesson

Teaching Tips and Suggestions:

What is an Insect? (page 7)

- The language in this Web site may be above some of the students' reading levels. Pair a stronger reader with someone who will need extra support. Give students the jobs of captain (who organizes and records answers) and navigator (who finds the information and reports).

Insect Body Parts (page 8)

- Read through the activity page together to make sure all students understand the questions and activities.
- Students will need to have at least one colored pencil or crayon to complete this page.

Insects A–Z (page 9)

- If students would like to learn more about an insect, they can click on that insect's picture.
- There are insect coloring pages on this site that you may allow students to print out.

Name_____

What is an Insect?

Go to **http://www.teachercreated.com/books/3408**

Click on **Page 7**, **Site 1**

1. How many body parts do insects have? _____

2. Name the body parts: the _____, the _____ (chest area), and the _____ (tail area).

❋ Click on the picture of the grasshopper on the Web site.   Label the picture below.

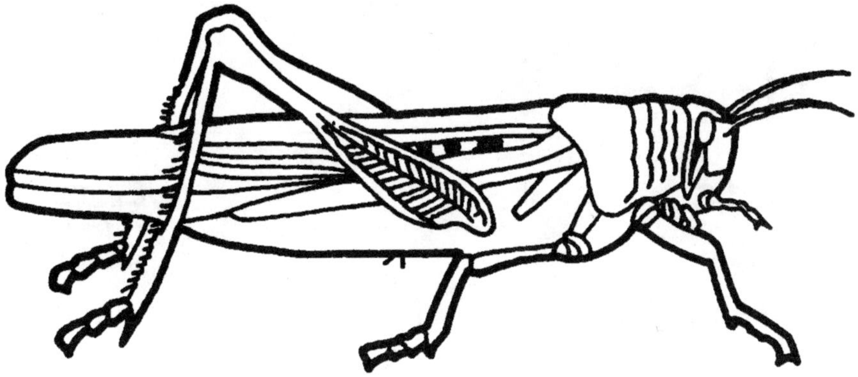

3. Describe what the grasshopper's wings look like. _____

_____

_____

4. Describe the grasshopper's legs. How are they different from your legs?

_____

_____

_____

Name _____

Insect Body Parts

Go to **http://www.teachercreated.com/books/3408**

Click on **Page 8**, **Site 1**

�֍ Read the description for each of the insect body parts below. Then, color the body part on the insect and write the body part on the line. The first one has been done for you.

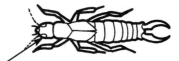

This part has the eyes, the antennae, and the mouth.

This can be a chewing type (grasshoppers and beetles) or a sucking type (aphids, butterflies, and moths).

1. ___ Head ___

4. _____

These are on the head and detect odors.

This is the middle body part with the legs attached to it.

2. _____

5. _____

This is the farthest end of the body from the head. It is made of 11 parts.

Adult insects have six of these. In some insects these are specially adapted for jumping.

3. _____

6. _____

Extra! Most insects have two pairs of _____.

Name_____

Insects A-Z

Go to **http://www.teachercreated.com/books/3408**

Click on **Page 9**, **Site 1**

✳ Read about insects and complete this activity
page.

1. Label the three main parts of this insect.

2. There are about _____ different types of insects.

3. Write down one name of an insect for each of the letters below.

A __**Ant**_____   O _____

B _____   P _____

D _____   Q _____

F _____   U _____

G _____   V _____

H _____   W_____

J_____   Y _____

L_____   Z _____

M _____

4. Click on one insect on the Web site. Get your teacher's permission to
print out that insect's coloring sheet.

Extra! This site does not list insects for every letter of the alphabet. See if
you can find insects that begin with these missing letters.

C _____   K _____   S _____

E _____   N _____   T _____

I _____   R _____   X _____

A Variety of Creepy Crawlies

Content Area(s):

- language
- science
- technology

Objectives:

In this section students:
- navigate their way around Web sites to find and record required information.
- identify the stages of insect metamorphosis.
- label insect body parts and sensory organs.
- differentiate between a spider and an insect.

Materials Required:

- computer with Internet access
- pencil or pen

Web Site(s):

- Students need to access the TCM Web page for the Creepy Crawlies book at:

http://www.teachercreated.com/books/3408

- Students then click on the link to the page on which they are working.
- Allow the children time to familiarize themselves with the Web site before starting the activity sheets.

Time:

- Approximately 30 minutes per lesson

Teaching Tips and Suggestions:

The Life of a Butterfly (page 11)

- This is an extensive Web site with plenty of support and activity suggestions for teachers.
- The concepts of a life cycle and metamorphosis should be addressed in class prior to doing this activity page.

A Louse and Some Lice (page 12)

- Whether you have students do the activity page alone or you work on it together, you will need to copy the images from the life cycle activity to a word processing document. Then, either print a copy for each student or use a large screen to display the entire life cycle.
- This activity can serve as a connection to a lesson on how to prevent the spread of head lice and to help children better understand what lice are.

Roach World (page 13)

- Tell children to pay attention to the circled numbers on the Web site to help them find the information.

EEK . . . a Spider! (page 14)

- Be sure to discuss with the students what they find out about spiders. You may want to do a Venn diagram comparing insects and spiders after doing the activity.

Name_____

The Life of a Butterfly

Go to **http://www.teachercreated.com/books/3408**

Click on **Page 11**, **Site 1**

❋ Draw a line from the picture to its description.

After some time, a butterfly comes out of the chrysalis.

The butterfly lays an egg on the leaf of a milkweed plant.

The caterpillar creates a chrysalis around its body.

A caterpillar is born. It eats the leaves of the plant for food.

❋ The life of a butterfly is sometimes looked at as a cycle. A cycle is something that happens over and over again. See if you can fill in the life cycle of the butterfly below by drawing pictures in the circles and labeling them.

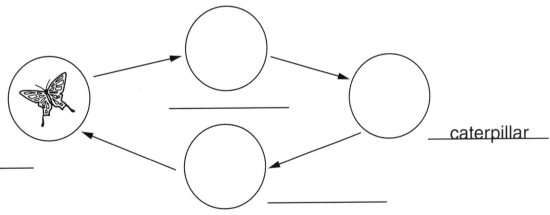

caterpillar

Extra! Check out some other links on the Web site.

Name _____

A Louse and Some Lice

Go to **http://www.teachercreated.com/books/3408**

Click on **Page 12**, **Site 1**

❃ Explore this *itchy* site to learn more about head lice.

A louse is what we call one of the bugs known as lice. Click on **Activities** and play **Hair Force One**. See how many lice you can zap.

1. How many lice did you zap on Level 1? _____

2. Play Level 2. How many lice did you zap in this game? _____

❃ Click on the **Animations** on the side screen and then click on the link for **The Life Cycle of a Louse**. Watch the pictures of a louse's life cycle. Then use the pictures your teacher gives you to draw and label the pictures of the louse for each stage below.

_____ **First Stage**	_____ **Second Stage**	_____ **Third Stage**
_____ **Fourth Stage**	__**Adult Male**__ **Final Stage**	__**Adult Female**__ **Final Stage**

❃ Next, click on the button that says **Poetry** and choose the **Sharing Poem**. Copy the poem on the lines below.

_____

_____

_____

_____

Name_____

Roach World

Go to **http://www.teachercreated.com/books/3408**

Click on **Page 13**, **Site 1**

❋ Label the parts of the cockroach below. Use the Web site to help you answer the questions about different parts of a cockroach's body.

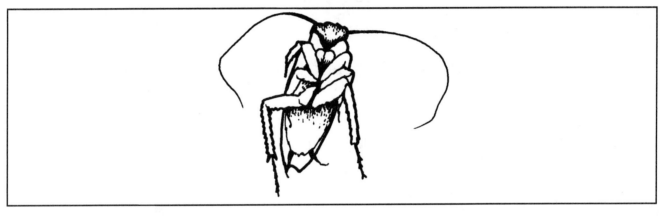

1. Antennae are used to _____ odors.

2. Thanks to their salivary glands, cockroaches can _____.

3. Hairs on cockroach legs are used for an extra sense of _____.

4. Each cockroach eye is made up of _____ lenses. Human eyes only have one lens.

5. A cockroach mouth can _____ as well as _____.

6. The two little hairs at the back of the cockroach that can tell when something is moving are called _____.

❋ Cockroaches eat at night and they love food! Think of two ways that you can help keep cockroaches away from your food when you are asleep at night.

➢ _____

➢ _____

> **Extra!** Visit some of the links on the Web site to learn more about "yucky" roaches.

Name _____

EEK . . . a Spider!

Go to **http://www.teachercreated.com/books/3408**

Click on **Page 14**, **Site 1**

❊ Explore the spider Web site to find answers for these questions.

1. Is a spider an insect? _____

2. What family do spiders belong to? _____

3. What are four other animals that also belong to this family?

   _____ _____ _____ _____

4. An insect has _____ legs and a spider has _____ legs.

   insect   **spider**

5. What kind of spider is in the first picture on this Web site? _____

6. Spiders have glands (very small organs) in their abdomens that make _____.

7. The silk is pushed out of the tube-like _____.

8. Spider webs are used to c_____ f_____ and to make c_____ to protect the young spiders.

❊ Click on the spider picture for a close-up look. Draw what you see in this box.

Extra! Click on the link to the **Butterfly and Bugs** page and have some fun!

Creepy Crawlies Everywhere!

Content Area(s):

- language
- science
- technology

Objectives:

In this section students:
- navigate their way around Web sites to find and record required information.
- identify the legs that go with certain insects and the characteristics that make them unique.
- draw and identify given insects.
- find an interesting fact about given insects from a Web site.

Materials Required:

- computer with Internet access
- pencil or pen

Web Site(s):

- Students need to access the TCM Web page for the Creepy Crawlies book at:

http://www.teachercreated.com/books/3408

- Students then click on the link to the page on which they are working.
- Allow the children time to familiarize themselves with the Web site before starting the activity sheets.

Time:

- Approximately 30 minutes per lesson

Teaching Tips and Suggestions:

Nice Legs! (page 16)

- The children will learn the functions of different insect legs through trial and error on the Web site, or you can discuss this with them before they go online. Be sure to follow up with a review of what they learned.
- Encourage students to explore the Web site and its links if they have time.

The Most Wanted (page 17)

- The pictures on this site are really colorful and wonderful. Let the children know that they just need to draw the general picture, not all the detail shown on the site.
- Point out that students can find out more about each insect by clicking on the individual pictures.

Get This Bug Off Of Me! (page 18)

- The language on this site is fairly complex, so ask children to find just one interesting thing about each creature. These facts can be found either in the pictures or in key words.

Name _____

Nice Legs!

Go to **http://www.teachercreated.com/books/3408**

Click on **Page 16**, **Site 1**

❋ Play the game to help each bug find its legs. In the boxes below, draw the creepy crawly and then write down an interesting fact about each one.

OR Ask your teacher if you can print out the coloring sheet at the end of the game. Then color and paste the bug pictures below.

_____

_____

_____

_____

_____

_____

_____

_____

Extra! Visit the **Activity Lab** at the bottom of the Web site and play another game!

Name_____

The Most Wanted

Go to **http://www.teachercreated.com/books/3408**

Click on **Page 17**, **Site 1**

❋ This site has lots of great pictures. You can click on each insect to see a bigger picture and find out more about the bug. (In case you did not know, AKA stands for "also known as.")

❋ Fill in the table below by drawing the bug and writing in the missing bug names.

Dog Flea	_____	_____
AKA: _____	AKA: _____Spot_____	AKA: ____Cruncher____
Black Ant	**Aphid Wasp**	_____
AKA: _____	AKA: _____	AKA: _____Juicy_____
_____	**Hammock Spider**	_____
AKA: _____Spike_____	AKA: _____	AKA: _____Buzzy_____

Name _____

Get This Bug Off Of Me!

Go to **http://www.teachercreated.com/books/3408**

Click on **Page 18**, **Site 1**

✤ Insects can be scary, but most of them won't hurt you.

1. Look at the insects that are NOT harmful. Draw a picture of each one below and then write one thing you learned about it on the fact lines.

Bug: _____**Daddy-Longlegs**_____

Fact: _____

_____

Bug: _____**Dragonfly**_____

Fact: _____

_____

2. Now look at the dangerous insects. Draw a picture and write one thing you learned about each of the creatures below.

Bug: _____**Tick**_____

Fact: _____

_____

Bug: _____**Black Widow**_____

Fact: _____

_____

Analyzing Bugs

Content Area(s):

- language
- science
- technology

Objectives:

In this section students:

- navigate their way around Alternet sites to find and record required information.
- identify insect body parts and sense organs.
- label the stages of bee metamorphosis.
- distinguish between insect and arachnid characteristics.

Materials Required:

- computer with Internet browser
- Alternet CD-ROM
- pencil or pen

Alternet:

- To use the Alternet CD-ROM, open [*begin.htm*]. For more instructions, see the section titled *How to Use the Alternet Program* on page 3.
- To go to individual pages, students access the index page and then click on the number of the page they are using.

Time:

- Approximately 30 minutes per lesson

Teaching Tips and Suggestions:

- The Alternet is a great place to begin teaching students about how to navigate Web sites on the World Wide Web. These activity sheets are also designed as an introduction to understanding insects and spiders.

Bug Study (page 20)

- You may want to do this page as a whole group to show students how to work on the Alternet and to cover the basics of insects.
- Emphasize that students need to focus on the pictures and colored words in addition to reading the text.

Spider or Insect? (page 21)

- Inform the students that some of the clues may be a little tricky so they will have to think before they answer.
- Preview the vocabulary of the body parts so students have a reference for pronunciation.

Name ______________________________

Bug Study

For this activity you will need the **Creepy Crawlies Alternet CD-ROM**.

Click on the link to **Page 20**.

1. A person who studies insects is called an ______________________________.
2. A skeleton on the outside, instead of the inside, is called an ____________.
3. All insects have _____________ legs and _____________ body parts.
4. Label the name of each insect body part on the picture below.

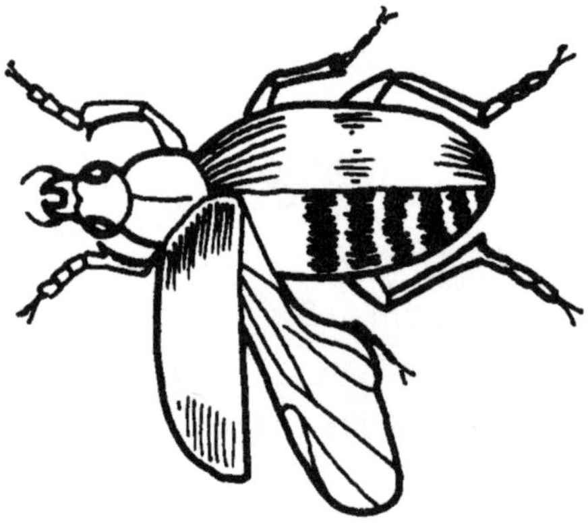

✽ Draw a line to show what a fly uses to do these things.

A fly tastes with . . .

A fly smells with . . .

A fly sees with . . .

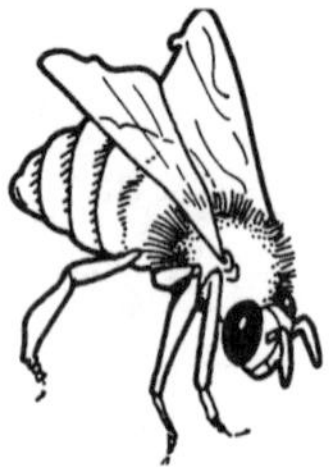

✽ Label each picture below to show the four stages of metamorphosis.

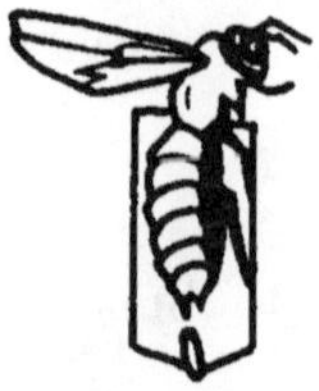

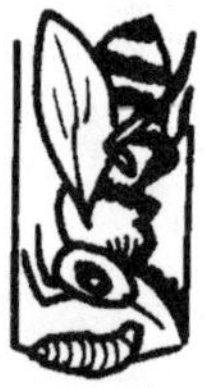

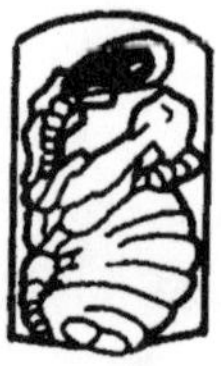

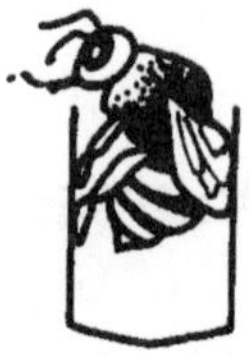

_______________ _______________ _______________ _______________

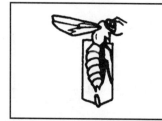

Name_____

Spider or Insect?

For this activity you will need the **Creepy Crawlies Alternet CD-ROM**.

Click on the link to **Page 21**.

1. Name four arachnids.

_____ _____ _____ _____

✽ How are spiders and insects different? For each clue below, write **I** if it is about insects, **S** if it is about spiders, and **B** if it is about both insects and spiders.

2. _____ have eight legs.

3. _____ usually have one or two pairs of wings.

4. _____ mostly eat insects.

5. _____ usually have eight simple eyes.

6. _____ smell with antennas.

7. _____ have one abdomen.

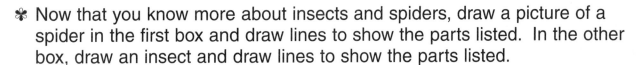

8. _____ sense with bristles on the legs.

9. _____ have two body parts.

✽ Now that you know more about insects and spiders, draw a picture of a spider in the first box and draw lines to show the parts listed. In the other box, draw an insect and draw lines to show the parts listed.

eyes

cephalothorax

abdomen

legs

spider	insect

antennae

compound eyes

head

abdomen

thorax

Beetles and Ladybugs

Content Area(s):

- language
- science
- technology

Objectives:

In this section students:

- navigate their way around Alternet sites to find and record required information.
- investigate and describe beetles.
- color different kinds of ladybugs.

Materials Required:

- computer with Internet browser
- Alternet CD-ROM
- pencil or pen

Alternet:

- To use the Alternet CD-ROM, open [*begin.htm*]. For more instructions, see the section titled *How to Use the Alternet Program* on page 3.
- To go to individual pages, students access the index page and then click on the number of the page they are using.

Time:

- Approximately 30 minutes per lesson

Teaching Tips and Suggestions:

- Both of these Alternet sites focus on beetles. You might want to go into greater depth about this large insect group.

Beautiful Beetles (page 23)

- Make sure that students understand what to do for the second part of the activity page. Provide an example on the board prior to allowing students into the computer lab. This activity can also be a fun way to practice spelling words or to write a story on a picture.

Ladybug, Ladybug (page 24)

- Ladybugs are the beetles with which students will probably be most familiar and comfortable. You may choose to bring some ladybugs into the class so that students can observe the wing covers and other features of beetles.
- Students should look at the bold print on the activity page for clues about where to find the required information.

Name_____

Beautiful Beetles

For this activity you will need the **Creepy Crawlies Alternet CD-ROM**.

Click on the link to **Page 23**.

1. Beetles live everywhere on earth except in the _____.

2. Why are beetles called the "armored tanks" of the insect world? _____

_____

_____

3. What are the special front wings of a beetle called? _____

✻ Find at least eight words to describe beetles. Write the words neatly around
the beetle picture below. Then color the beetle.

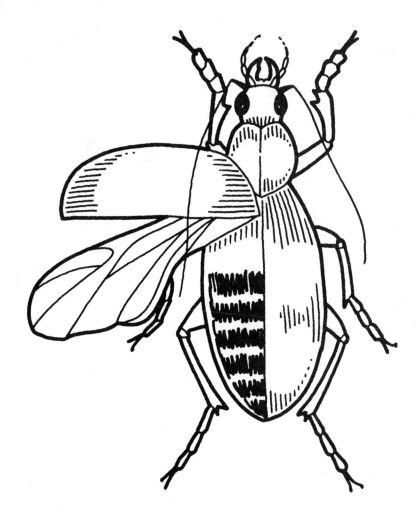

Name _____

Ladybug, Ladybug

For this activity you will need the **Creepy Crawlies Alternet CD-ROM**.

Click on the link to **Page 24**.

1. What is the real name for the ladybug? _____

2. How many different kinds of ladybugs live in the United States? _____

❋ Read about the **Pretty Colors** of ladybugs. Color four different ladybugs.

3. Name one reason why predators do not like to eat ladybugs.

_____

4. What is the name of the insect that ladybugs like to eat? _____

5. Who is the ladybug named after? _____

6. What is a baby ladybug called? _____

Your Neighborhood Creepy Crawlies

Content Area(s):

- language
- science
- technology

Objectives:

In this section students:

- navigate their way around Alternet sites to find and record required information.
- research and record the life of a worker bee.
- make decisions and form opinions based on given information.
- identify differences between short- and long-horned grasshoppers.

Materials Required:

- computer with Internet browser
- Alternet CD-ROM
- pencil or pen

Alternet:

- To use the Alternet CD-ROM, open [*begin.htm*]. For more instructions see the section titled *How to Use the Alternet Program* on page 3.
- To go to individual pages, students access the index page and then click on the number of the page they are using.

Time:

- Approximately 30 minutes per lesson

Teaching Tips and Suggestions:

Busy Bees (page 26)

- There is a lot more to the lives of bees than is provided here. You may want to make an extension to the social aspect of some insects' lives and compare/contrast them to human societies.

The Ants Go Marching (page 27)

- Ants are also social insects. Try starting an ant farm for the class to observe and enjoy.
- You might also choose to do an activity on weight to help students better understand the strength of ants.

Hoppy to Know You (page 28)

- You may choose to do an activity where pairs of students use different measurement units to see how long 100 feet actually is.

Name _____

Busy Bees

For this activity you will need the **Creepy Crawlies Alternet CD-ROM**.

Click on the link to **Page 26**.

✽ Read about **Busy Bees** to learn more about these amazing insects.

1. Bees are valued for making _____ and for helping _____ flowers and plants.

2. What are four things kept in the six-sided cells in a hive?

   _____ _____ _____ _____

3. Which bee is the most important bee in the hive? _____

4. Describe the lives of worker bees in the chart below:

Days 1–3: _____

Days 4–9: _____

Days 10–15: _____

Days 16–20: _____

Days 21+: _____

5. What is the yellow powder in flowers called? _____

✽ Pretend that you have a glass-walled bee hive. Draw what you might see happening inside of the hive.

Name_____

The Ants Go Marching

For this activity you will need the **Creepy Crawlies Alternet CD-ROM**.

Click on the link to **Page 27**.

1. A group of insects that live together is called a _____.

2. Name three things that rooms in an ant nest are used for:

   _____

   _____

   _____

3. Would you rather be a boy ant or a girl ant? Why?

   _____

   _____

4. Name some things that you could lift if you were as strong as an ant.

   _____

   _____

✽ For each line below, write the ant that gets its food in these ways:

Army ants	**Slave makers**	**Harvester ants**
Dairying ants	**Honey ants**	**Fungus growers**

5. _____ need slaves to feed them and work for them.

6. _____ make gardens and grow fungus.

7. _____ collect seeds and chew them into ant bread.

8. _____ hang a fat ant from the ceiling to throw up honeydew.

9. _____ have soldiers that kill any creature that can't get away.

10. _____ get honeydew from aphids and plant lice.

Name _____

Hoppy to Know You

For this activity you will need the **Creepy Crawlies Alternet CD-ROM**.

Click on the link to **Page 28**.

1. How far could you hop if you could hop like a grasshopper? _____

2. Name two types of short-horned grasshoppers.

   _____   _____

3. The difference between short- and long-horned grasshoppers is the length
   of their _____.

4. Name two kinds of long-horned grasshoppers.

   _____

   _____

5. Draw a line from the color of the grasshopper to where it lives.

   green   **brown**   **sandy**

6. How many eyes does a grasshopper have? _____

7. How long does it take for a grasshopper to become an adult? _____

8. What is it called when a grasshopper loses its outside skeleton and grows a
   bigger new one? _____

9. How do grasshoppers "sing"? _____

   _____

Interesting Facts About Bugs

Content Area(s):

- language
- science
- technology

Objectives:

In this section students:

- navigate their way around Alternet sites to find and record required information.
- identify given insects as helpful or harmful.
- create a menu of insects that are eaten by people.
- answer questions about insects.

Materials Required:

- computer with Internet browser
- Alternet CD-ROM
- pencil or pen

Alternet:

- To use the Alternet CD-ROM, open [*begin.htm*]. For more instructions see the section titled *How to Use the Alternet Program* on page 3.
- To go to individual pages, students access the index page and then click on the number of the page they are using.

Time:

- Approximately 30 minutes per lesson

Teaching Tips and Suggestions:

The Good, the Bad, and the Creepy (page 30)

- Discuss how some insects can be both helpful and harmful.

Yummy Bugs (page 31)

- Have an insect party that includes insect foods. If you or the children are uncomfortable with eating insects, there are also options of forming more commonly eaten foods, such as biscuits, into insect shapes.

Interesting Insects (page 32)

- This section on the Alternet has many interesting facts about various insects. You might want to make a class list of interesting insect facts that the children find as they research.

Name ______________________________

The Good, the Bad, and the Creepy

For this activity you will need the **Creepy Crawlies Alternet CD-ROM**.

Click on the link to **Page 30**.

❃ Look at the insects below and circle whether they are helpful and/or harmful. In the box, write how each insect helps and/or harms people.

ladybug helpful harmful

bee helpful harmful

termite helpful harmful

fly helpful harmful

butterfly helpful harmful

spider helpful harmful

Name_____

Yummy Bugs

For this activity you will need the **Creepy Crawlies Alternet CD-ROM**.

Click on the link to **Page 31**.

❋ Fill in the Insect Menu with the insects that are eaten or the part of the world that eats the insects. Then, make up your own insect dish for the "Special of the Day."

Insect Menu

Country	Insect Food
_____	Delicious Bagong moths cooked in hot ashes with their wings removed **OR** crunchy cooked Witchetty grubs
Japan	Hachi-No-Ko: _____ _____: water insect larvae Inago: _____
Nigeria, Africa	_____
_____	Dragonflies grilled with ginger, garlic, shallots, coconut milk, and a hint of chili pepper.
Special of the Day	_____ _____

❋ Would you rather eat food with little bits of insects in it or food that has dangerous chemicals in it? Explain your answer.

_____

_____

_____

Name _____

Interesting Insects

For this activity you will need the **Creepy Crawlies Alternet CD-ROM**.

Click on the link to **Page 32**.

1. What is the name of the fossil dragonfly that lived over 250 million years ago?

   _____

2. Which insects are the fastest runners?

   _____

3. How many eggs can a queen termite lay every day?

   _____

4. How long does it take an aphid baby to become an adult?

   _____

5. How do butterflies close their wings?

   _____

6. How do moths close their wings?

   _____

7. *True or False:* Monarch butterflies stop in the same trees every year when they fly south for the winter.

   _____

8. *True or False:* A firefly is actually a beetle.

   _____

9. What is the longest insect in the world?

   _____

Comparing and Collecting Bugs

Content Area(s):

- reading and comprehension
- science
- research

Objectives:

In this section students:

- use resource materials to find required information.
- differentiate between insects and non-insects.
- identify insect homes.
- practice creating an image with bilateral symmetry.

Materials Required:

- library, computer, or other resource materials
- pencil or pen, old magazines, glue, scissors

Time:

- Approximately 30 minutes per lesson

Teaching Tips and Suggestions:

Which One is an Insect? (page 34)

- Review the attributes of insects (six legs, wings usually, and three body parts) before allowing students to do the activity. Have reference books, encyclopedias, or computers available for students to research creatures of which they are unsure.

Home Sweet Home (page 35)

- Take a nature walk and look for insect homes around the school or neighborhood.

The Same on Both Sides (page 36)

- Follow this with an art activity where you give each student a piece of paper with half of a butterfly shape printed in the middle. Have them fold it in half and cut. When they open it, both sides should be exactly the same shape. You may then assist children in putting drops of paint on one side. When the butterfly is folded over, pressed together, and opened up, both sides will be the same pattern, showing bilateral symmetry.

Bug Collection (page 37)

- Provide many magazines and reference books for children to use to find insect names.

Name _____

Which One is an Insect?

❋ Use your library or other resources to help you complete this activity page.

❋ Remember that all insects have three body parts (head, thorax, and abdomen) and three pairs of legs. Look at the list below. Decide which are insects and which are not insects.

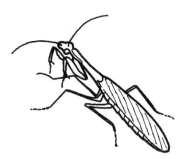

earthworm	butterfly	earwig
bee	mouse	scorpion
lizard	mosquito	louse (lice)
aphid	housefly	hummingbird
crab	spider	cricket
cockroach	snail	centipede

INSECT	NOT AN INSECT
_____	_____
_____	_____
_____	_____
_____	_____
_____	_____
_____	_____
_____	_____
_____	_____
_____	_____

❋ Now, write three of your own insects and three things that are not insects.

_____	_____
_____	_____
_____	_____

Name_____

Home Sweet Home

✤ Insects live in different types of homes. Find out what type of home each of these insects lives in. Draw a line from the insect to its home.

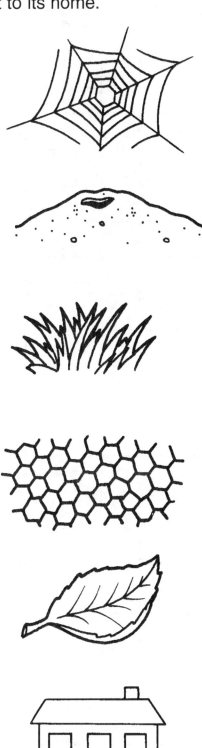

Name _____

The Same on Both Sides

✳ Insects have what we call *bilateral symmetry*. That means that they are
exactly the same on both sides of their bodies. Draw the other half of each
insect below to show the *bilateral symmetry*.

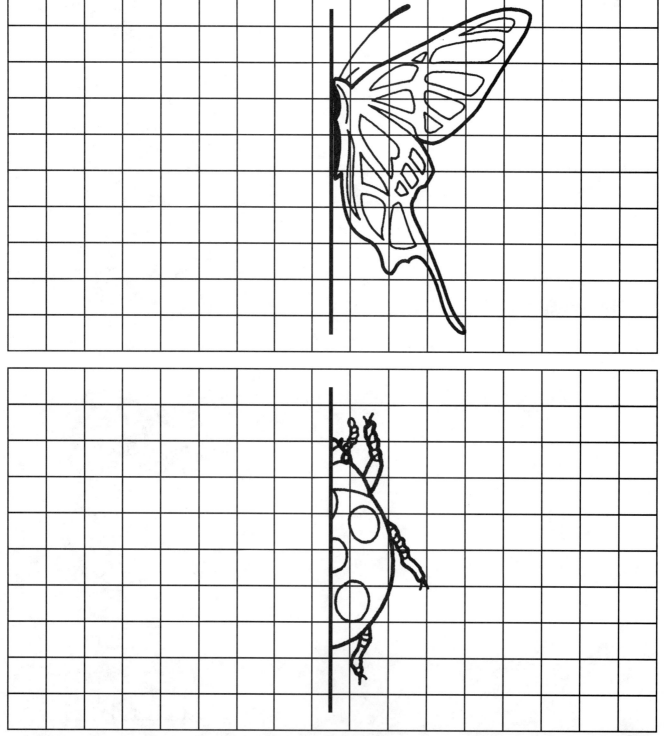

Name_____

Bug Collection

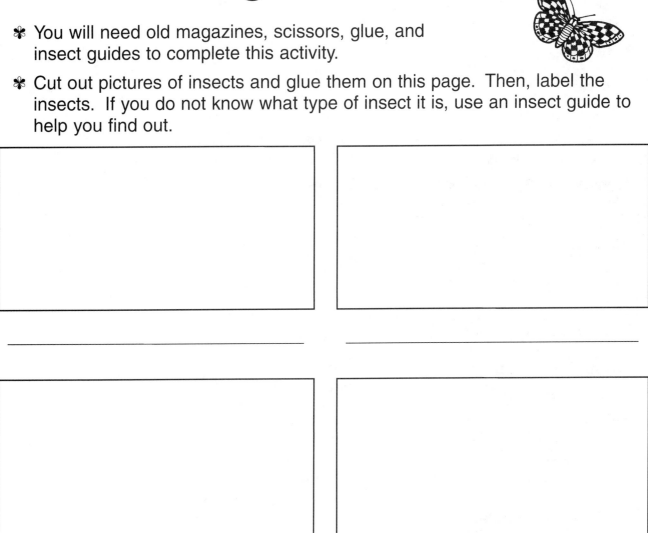

✻ You will need old magazines, scissors, glue, and insect guides to complete this activity.

✻ Cut out pictures of insects and glue them on this page. Then, label the insects. If you do not know what type of insect it is, use an insect guide to help you find out.

Fun with Games

Content Area(s):

- reading and comprehension
- spelling
- research

Objectives:

In this section students:

- use resource materials to find information as needed.
- find insect words in a word search.
- complete a crossword puzzle with insect clues and answers.

Materials Required:

- library, computer, or other resource materials
- pencil

Time:

- Approximately 30 minutes per lesson

Teaching Tips and Suggestions:

Bug Search (page 39)

- Preview how to do a word search. Assist students with finding the first one or two words. You might want to allow them to work in small groups. Students can either circle the words in the puzzle or lightly color over each.
- After students complete the puzzle, talk about different methods that students used for the activity.

Cross-Bug Puzzle (page 40)

- Preview how to do a crossword puzzle with the students. You may opt to do this as a whole group activity.
- Help students read through the clues and answers before attempting the puzzle.

Name_____

Bug Search

❋ Can you find all of the insect words in this word search? Look for and circle
or color the answers that go across, up and down, or diagonal.

insect	sting	thorax	head	ladybug	larva
egg	itch	abdomen	bee	mosquito	lice
ant	six legs	spider	flea	earwig	moth
wings	pupa	antenna	beetle	wasp	dragonfly

M	O	S	Q	U	I	T	O	B	B	K
I	N	S	E	C	T	H	B	E	E	Q
P	U	P	A	B	D	O	M	E	N	E
H	W	I	N	G	S	R	A	T	N	W
E	A	R	W	I	G	A	F	L	E	A
A	N	T	J	S	I	X	L	E	G	S
D	R	A	G	O	N	F	L	Y	G	P
L	A	R	V	A	S	P	I	D	E	R
A	N	T	E	N	N	A	C	T	Z	X
L	A	D	Y	B	U	G	E	V	C	F
S	T	I	N	G	J	K	M	O	T	H

Extra! Try to make your own word search with bug names on a piece of
graph paper. Give it to a friend to try to complete.

Name _____

Cross-Bug Puzzle

✴ Use the clues at the bottom of the page to put the bug names from the box in the crossword puzzle.

beetle	
termite	
butterfly	
cricket	
mosquito	
flea	
bee	
ant	
moth	
spider	
lice	

Across

2. I have eight legs. I am an arachnid, not an insect.
3. I eat wood.
5. Some people think that I look like a flower flying in the sky.
8. I look like a butterfly and fly at night.
9. If you have a picnic, I will come to steal crumbs
10. I am sometimes called the "armored tank" of insects.

Down

1. You will have an itchy head if we get in your hair.
4. You itch after I bite you.
6. I rub my legs together to make noise.
7. I make your dog or cat itch.
10. I make a sweet treat that you might like to eat.

What Do You Know?

Content Area(s):

- reading and comprehension
- science
- research

Objectives:

In this section students:

- use resource materials to find information as needed.
- follow multi-step directions.
- identify helpful and harmful insects.
- choose, research, and record information on an insect.

Materials Required:

- library, computer, or other resource materials
- pencil and crayons

Time:

- Approximately 30 minutes per lesson

Teaching Tips and Suggestions:

Stop Bugging Me! (page 42)

- If students are unsure about whether or not an insect is helpful or harmful, they may need to use a reference to find out. Make reference materials available and discuss how and when students can use them.
- Circulate around the room and allow students to justify their reasoning to you.

My Favorite Insect (page 43)

- Preview how to use reference materials to find information on a subject.
- This activity should come toward the end of a unit of study on bugs.
- You could create a display showing the students' favorite creepy crawlies. You might also graph the results if there appears to be some popular insects and spiders.

Name _____

Stop Bugging Me!

Some insects are helpful, some are harmful, and some are just a bother.

✻ Color the helpful insects and circle the harmful insects. Then, put an **X** over each insect that "bugs" you.

Name_____

My Favorite Insect

Use your library, a computer, or other resources to help you complete this page.

❊ There are many different insects in the world. Which one is your favorite? Find out more about one special insect.

My favorite insect is _____

❊ Draw and color a picture of your insect in the box.

➢ It eats _____

➢ It gets food by _____

➢ It lives _____

➢ It moves by _____

➢ It is helpful to people when it _____

➢ It is harmful to people when it _____

➢ I like this insect because _____

_____

Writing About Bugs

Content Area(s):

- reading, writing, and comprehension
- science
- research

Objectives:

In this section students:

- use resource materials to find information as needed.
- use their knowledge about insects to create a unique insect.
- write a story about what it would be like to have insect abilities.

Materials Required:

- library, computer, or other resource materials
- pencil and crayons

Time:

- Approximately 30 minutes per lesson

Teaching Tips and Suggestions:

New Insect Discovered! (page 45)

- Preview how to use reference materials to find information on a subject.
- Model this activity by helping students brainstorm what might happen if you mixed a butterfly with a ladybug (butterbug) or a spider with a fly (spiderfly). What might the insect eat, where would it live, how would it get food, would it be helpful or harmful, etc.
- Explain that new insects are being discovered all of the time, especially in rain forests and jungles. Have them think about a new insect and describe its characteristics.

Bug Power! (page 46)

- Review some of the activities associated with ants and grasshoppers. Perhaps read a story about someone with extra-human strength.
- Go over the directions for the activity and have students talk about some of their ideas.
- You may want students to do their "best guess" spelling on a sheet of lined paper for the first draft and then edit it and write it on the activity page for a final draft. You could combine the stories into a class book.

Name_____

New Insect Discovered!

✽ Pretend that you are an entomologist (person who studies insects) and have just discovered a new insect. Use what you know about insects and make up your very own insect. Complete this fact sheet to share your insect with the world.

➤ Insect Name: _____

Draw and color a
picture of the insect.

➤ Where the insect lives: _____

➤ What the insect eats: _____

➤ How the insect gets food: _____

_____

➤ How the insect gets around: _____

_____

➤ How the insect helps people: _____

_____

➤ How the insect harms people: _____

_____

➤ Other interesting things about the insect: _____

_____

_____

Name _____

Bug Power!

✳ If you could jump like a grasshopper and lift as much weight as an ant, you would be able to jump over 100 feet and lift a car! Write a story about a day that you wake up and have the power of an insect. What might happen? What sorts of things would you do? Draw a picture for your story in the box.

Extra! Think of ways that you could measure 100 feet on the playground.
Have a friend or teacher help you try it out.

Answer Key

Page 7—What is an Insect?
1. three; 2. head, thorax, abdomen; 3-4. Answers will vary.

Page 8—Insect Body Parts
1. head; 2. antennae; 3. abdomen; 4. mouth; 5. thorax; 6. legs.

Page 9—Insects A–Z
1. head, thorax, abdomen; 2. a million; 3. Answers will vary.

Page 11—The Life of a Butterfly
Egg = The butterfly lays an egg on the leaf of a milkweed plant; *Larva* = A caterpillar is born. It eats the leaves of the plant for food; *Pupa* = The caterpillar creates a chrysalis around its body; *Butterfly* = After some time, a butterfly comes out of the chrysalis.

Page 12—A Louse and Some Lice
1-2. Answers will vary. Stages are: egg (nit), 1st nymph, 2nd nymph, 3rd nymph, Adult male, Adult female; Sharing Poem = It's OK to share. Share a toy, share a slide, share the feelings deep inside, but never share a hat or comb, or lice could make your head their home.

Page 13—Roach World
1. smell; 2. spit; 3. touch; 4. 2,000; 5. smell, taste; 6. cerci

Page 14—EEK . . . A Spider!
1. no; 2. arachnid; 3. scorpions, ticks, daddy longlegs, and mites; 4 six, eight; 5. tarantula; 6. silk; 7. spinnaret; 8. catch food, cocoons.

Page 16—Nice Legs!
Answers will vary.

Page 17—The Most Wanted
Dog Flea = Ukelele; Ladybug = Spot; Termite = Cruncher; Black Ant = Hercules; Aphid Wasp = Little Al; Fruit Fly = Juicy; Mosquito = Spike; Hammock Spider = Spinner; House Fly = Buzzy.

Page 18—Get This Bug Off Of Me!
Answers will vary.

Page 20—Bug Study
1. entomologist; 2. exoskeleton; 3. six, three; 4. (See student work); Flies taste with their feet, smell with their legs, and see with compound eyes; Metamorphosis pictures are: egg, larva, pupa, and adult.

Page 21—Spider or Insect?
1. scorpions, ticks, spiders, daddy longlegs, or mites; 2. Spiders; 3. Insects; 4. Spiders; 5. Spiders; 6. Insects; 7. Both; 8. Spiders; 9. Spiders.

Page 23—Beautiful Beetles
1. oceans; 2. They have a hard wing cover and an exoskeleton to protect them; 3. Elytra.

Page 24—Ladybug, Ladybug
1. ladybird beetle; 2. About 150; 3. Answers will vary; 4. aphid; 5. Jesus' mother Mary; 6. grub.

Page 26—Busy Bees
1. honey, pollinate; 2. honey, pollen, eggs, and larvae; 3. the queen bee; 4. Days 1–3 clean the hive, Days 4–9 feed the larvae, Days 10–15 build new hive cells, Days 16–20 make honey, Days 21+ guard the hive and collect nectar and pollen; 5. pollen.

Page 27—The Ants Go Marching
1. colony; 2. storing food, caring for the young, the queen; 3-4. Answers will vary; 5. Slave makers; 6. Fungus growers; 7. Harvester ants; 8. Honey ants; 9. Army ants; 10. Dairying ants.

Answer Key (cont.)

Page 28—Hoppy to Know You
1. 100 feet; 2. lubber grasshoppers and locusts; 3. antennae; 4. katydids and mormon crickets; 5. green = trees and leaves, brown = grass and ground, sandy = beach; 6. five; 7. 40-60 days; 8. molting; 9. by rubbing their legs together.

Page 30—The Good, The Bad, and The Creepy
Ladybug = helpful: eats pests such as aphids; Bee = helpful: pollinates plants, harmful: stings; Termite = harmful: attacks furniture and wood; Fly = harmful: spreads germs; Butterfly = helpful: pollinates plants; Spider = helpful: eats other insect pests, harmful: bites.

Page 31—Yummy Bugs
Australia; boiled wasp larvae; Zaza-mushi; fried grasshopper; Bali; Answers will vary.

Page 32—Interesting Insects
1. Meganeura; 2. cockroaches; 3. 6,000–7,000; 4. one week; 5. back to back; 6. in a tent shape; 7. True; 8. True; 9. giant stick insect.

Page 34—Which One is an Insect?
Insect: aphid, butterfly, housefly, earwig, bee, cricket, cockroach, mosquito, louse; Not an Insect: earthworm, hummingbird, crab, mouse, spider, scorpion, lizard, snail, centipede.

Pages 35–37
Answers will vary

Page 39

M	O	S	Q	U	I	T	O	B	B	K
I	N	S	E	C	T	H	B	E	E	Q
P	U	P	A	B	D	O	M	E	N	E
H	W	I	N	G	S	R	A	T	N	W
E	A	R	W	I	G	A	F	L	E	A
A	N	T	J	S	I	X	L	E	G	S
D	R	A	G	O	N	F	L	Y	G	P
L	A	R	V	A	S	P	I	D	E	R
A	N	T	E	N	N	A	C	T	Z	X
L	A	D	Y	B	U	G	E	V	C	F
S	T	I	N	G	J	K	M	O	T	H

Page 40—Cross-Bug Puzzle
1. lice; 2. spider; 3. termite; 4. mosquito; 5. butterfly; 6. cricket; 7. flea; 8. moth; 9. ant; 10a. beetle; 10d. bee.

Page 42–46
Answers will vary.